EVEN

IF MY

HANDS

WERE

FULL

Sherell Watson

EVEN IF MY HANDS WERE FULL

Sherell Watson

Sherell Watson is a proud Brooklynite. With the intention of eventually saving lives, she started her collegiate career attending the historic Morris Brown College in Atlanta, GA as a biology major before realizing literature could be an equally powerful healer, thus leading Sherell to obtain her Baccalaureate of Arts in English Literature at Benedict College in Columbia, SC. There, she crafted and honed her writing ability while interning for a local newspaper, *Black News*, and as the Entertainment Editor of *The Tiger News*, all the while being of service as a proud member of Zeta Phi Beta Sorority, Inc. When she's not chasing summer with her favorite person, her son, Sherell can be found writing, reading, laughing, and living her best life in her hometown, Brooklyn, NY.

© Copyright Sherell Watson 2020

ISBN: 978-0-578-76530-3
Printed in the United States of America
First Printing, 2020

For my favorite person, my chocolate drop, my son,
Corey J. Watson

Contents

I

II

I

ACKNOWLEDGEMENTS

First and foremost, I would like to thank God for all He has done and all He continues to do in my life. Thereafter lies a mile-long list starting with my parents, Geraldine and Marty. Mom, thank you for always letting me know I have a voice, allowing me to utilize it and letting me know that when I couldn't speak the words, I could always write them. Dad, thank you for always supporting me, loving me, providing for me, and encouraging me in all my efforts. The piece of papyrus you were cut from, they don't make it anymore. Love you both ALWAYS.

I want to thank my sisters, Sheriee, Kashonda, Katasha and Nateshia, thank you ladies for ALWAYS being there through everything. Thank you for providing a listening ear, loving support, advice, and encouragement. Thank you for loving me the way only y'all do. Thank you for being my anchors when I've been drifting and the scissors when I've been weighed down. The amount of love I have for you ladies is immeasurable.

Throughout my life, I've encountered individuals who have left an indelible mark on it and those individuals have become family to me, so thank you Sonya Goddard, Latiya Stanley, Marquita A. Watson-Roberts and Jessica E. Green for providing unlimited support, guidance, love, advice, compassion, and understanding, no matter the time or distance. Knowing I have you in my corner, I feel invincible.

To my family, the Watsons, the Powells, the Robinsons, the Wallaces, Elka Balboda and the Profits, thank you for the continued love and support. Family is everything! We all we got! Love all y'all to the moon and back.

Thank you, Kallie Falandays of Tell Tell Poetry, for your guidance, support, and knowledge during this process, I will be forever grateful.

Finally to my Angels, my grandmother Julia Watson, my uncle Robert Watson Jr., my father Vernal L. Robinson, and my grandfather Robert Watson Sr. I miss you, love you and thank you for guiding and keeping me. I feel your presence and eternal love always.

DEAR READER

Sitting here contemplating, wondering if you're feeling the same way.
Confused about the love I have for you, wondering if your love is the same.
Needing you to *Show me you feel the same way too.*
Holding you in my arms, feeling each beat of my blood trying to reach you,
loving you with my soul.
These feelings I have for you, I'll never control.
I love you.
I love you.
I'll say it again,
I love you.
I love you from deep within.

MY BED

I bought it long before I met you.
I took my time to pick it.
I labored over this decision,
figuring out the spacing, the placement, the utility, the durability, the look,
    the wood, the curves.
Tried to figure out if I would be comfortable.
I purchased its accessory with the same vigor, deliberating, trying,
    testing to see what fit me and my needs.

It has served me well.

I've laid in it countless nights alone with my thoughts.
I've laid in it with my child on my chest to put him to sleep.
I've laid in it in physical pain, in the grips of sickness.
I've laid in it, crying tears from grief.
I've laid in it and written the words from my soul.
I've laid in it alone with my thoughts and fears and dreams and goals.
I've rolled around and dreamed big dreams.
I've washed it down, rearranged it, moved it around, found my Zen spot.
I've laid in it and entertained, made men and women say my name,
describe in detail how I'm making them feel.
I've laid in it and felt the purest pleasure and the sweetest pain.
I've laid in it, and I've slept on all sides.

But, as of today, my haven has become uncomfortable to say the least.
I've slept in the middle, on the left, and on the right,
alone, with my child, or special company, and my bed has felt as unfamiliar
    to me
as a white person's potato salad or mac and cheese.
You've only spent minimal time in my place of peace, but you have changed
    it irrevocably
and have unglued my world,

unbalanced my beam,
unhinged my door and made me see
that, being with a man like you, it's a hard thing to choose
between loving yourself and having nothing left to lose.

I WISH I COULD SLEEP LIKE EVERYONE ELSE

I wish I could sleep like everyone else,
then I'd dream all my troubles away.

That's never the case, so I'm up yet again, watching night turn into day.

GOING CRAZY

An amputee misses their legs. I miss you.
I still can't understand how I let you get so deep inside my head, my heart,
    my soul.
Because of all that, it's hard to let you go.
I find myself sitting, reflecting, reminiscing on all the good shit.
I thought I had found a good nigga in the hood.
But that ain't you, and this ain't me.
I'm not the type to sit and dwell constantly about some nigga who didn't
    do me no good.
So why am I doing it?
Why do I care?
Why do I sit and stare at the places we've stood and talked?
Why do I walk to the places we've walked?
Why do I check the places you usually be?
Cause somewhere, deep down inside,
I know you're doing the same.
Hopefully.

PANDORA'S BOX

Hope doesn't give a fuck.
Hope dims your light, making you see things
that aren't there.

When will you ever quit?
Hope is the most detrimental beast she left us with.

I've given all I can.
I've put up with so much
dealing with all your drama; it's all too much.

My heart has been broken.
You're the love of my life, yet you have me broken
down into the smallest particles.
I'm reduced to nothing but a token.
No longer do I wear the crown.
My castle has been destroyed.
It's nothing but pieces.

You have the key to unlock the doors.
You're the layer of my bricks.
My foundation isn't solid unless you're in the mix.
Only you have the key.
My heart belongs only to you; you only have to speak.
Yet you speak in codes and clues when you speak at all. Hope,
the most detrimental emotion, that's what she left us with.
Hope keeps me thinking we're not done yet.
Hope makes me want you when I know you're no good.
Hope makes me have dreams of me and you.
Hope keeps me going when there's nothing left to say.
Hope is Zeus laughing at the peoples' curse
because Pandora held onto the worst of the worst.

Hope dims you;
it's the stealer of time,
yet you don't even care.
You smile, speak, and stare;
hope is all I have, and I can't care.

RIDE

I'm feeling erratic
something's taking over me.
I can't hold it.
I can't control it,
so I let go
and let him control me.

I can't hide it.
I can't fight it,
so I give in and hold tight.
I let him dip and dive,
slip and slide,
and I just hold on with all my might.
This ride never ends
because, as soon as we stop, we roll over and do it again.

MY LOVE FOR YOU IS EVER FLOWING, NEVER DYING LIKE THE RIVER NILE

My love for you is ever flowing, never dying like the river Nile.
My love for you is ever growing, forever full like roses in bloom.
My love for you is never faltering; just like the perfect musician, my love is
   always in tune.

The love I have for you emerges slowly from my eyes.
The love I have for you expresses itself in these tears I cry.

I WANT YOU

I wrote something once for this guy.
I constructed multiple sentences, then remembered my training.
I added nuance and symbolism and tried to spice it up with a little
  alliteration.
I grabbed the dictionary and rifled its pages.
I read a Shakespearean sonnet, tried to mimic his cadence.
I played Scrabble with various words and placements,
all in hope that he would understand the simplest of phrases:

I WANT YOU.

GHOSTED

Why'd you have to go
when I was feeling you just so?
I thought we had something good, you know?
I'm digging you.
You digging me.
Shit, that feeling was sweet.
But you haven't called, and I don't know why.
Was it something I said? Something I did?
I don't know what to think.
You see you got me sitting here contemplating what could have been,
wondering, did I miss my only chance?
Did I get just a glimpse or a glance of what love was?
Shit, I wonder now if we even had a chance?
But the thoughts are overwhelmed by the fact that you're confused.
So confused you can't even call.
I wonder why I bothered at all.
Starting to care.
Starting to get used to your voice.
Starting to wonder if I made the right choice in revealing the things I did.
Wondering if you were the right man.
Wondering if I finally stood a chance at finding out what love was all about.
Promising I'd never hurt you and, in return, you doing the same.
So now I know because of what you've done,
that truly you are not The One.

MORNING AFTER

When my face is glowing and the sky is pouring down beams of glorious
    light,
what will you think of me?

I just gave you my resounding all without a fight,
let you deep inside my walls. . . .

You crawled in, then lay there for eternity, loving me from the inside out.
But today's a new day,

and it's the morning after,
and my laughter is silenced by doubt.

What will you think of me?

I JUST DON'T UNDERSTAND HOW I CAN WANT YOU SO BAD

I just don't understand how I can want you so bad and need you so much,
and you're not even my man.
How, with the slightest touch, you send chills down my spine and my breath
catches and my pulse races when I look you in the eyes,
and I don't disguise the feelings I have for you,

the need, the desire to hold you in my arms as if I were your woman and the
only one you need and love.
Maybe, in time, it'll be true.
Maybe the feelings I have, you'll feel them too.
Maybe one day I'll see more than lust in your eyes and your face will fill with
surprise because you've seen me for the woman I am.
Your woman.
The one you seek for advice and love and comfort and heat in the darkest
hour.
I could be your woman.
I could be that woman.
All the powers are invested in me,
but you have yet to really look at me.

THE SUN RISES AND SETS ON YOU

The sun rises and sets on you.
Cloudy days went away with you.
Words are never enough to show I care.
Not having you to hold, to touch, is too much to bear.
My heart is sore thinking about this loss.
I'm always in control of my emotions,
but you've taken a notion to take your love from me, and now I feel like I'm
 going crazy.

What do I have to do?
What do I have to say to make you feel the same way?
Cause when I'm with you, nothing is more important than the time we
 spend together.
I've never felt safer than when I'm in your arms,
sharing daily thoughts that are on my mind,
and it feels good knowing you took the time to consider what I've been
 through.
But we're through,
and I never wanted to feel this way,
walking, talking, breathing, living without you.

What do I have to do?
What do I have to say to make you feel the same way?

Right now our love is one-sided, not flowing both ways and all I can do is
 reminisce
on the days when it did, and we were a team.
But all that is gone now, and reality is making those moments fizzle like a
 distant dream.

What do I have to do?
What do I have to say to make you feel the same way?

Because even though we're through,
you're the love of my life,
and I'll always, always, always love you.

ODE TO BABY MOMMAS

Cold, cold I feel all the way in my spirit.
The tears are flowing, these I can't control.
My heart is aching to be with that one.
The one who left me high and dry under the burning sun.
He left me there naked and bare.
Alone and lonely.
Alone in despair.
I told him my feelings; he'd wanted to know.
I'd told him I loved him, he said he'd never let me go.

But he pushed me to the side, speeding off in his new fly ride.
He left me on the highway alone.
Cold and naked to the bone, stripped of my dignity, and pride.
Stripped of the seat of OUR new fly ride.
He said I was the one eternally, but then she came along, and I was the bum,
    the bitch, the whore,
the one he couldn't stand no more.
This highway I walk, we were supposed to walk together.

I walk it alone now but this storm I'll weather.
These tears will dry; I will no longer cry.
My heart will get stronger; I'll need you no longer.
With my pride intact, I'll straighten my back and hold my head high,
because I don't need a bum standing by my side.
I won't look for my new man; he'll look for me.
All the good things you overlooked,
he'll see.

I'M UGLY ON THE INSIDE THEREFORE I'M UGLY ON THE OUTSIDE

I'm ugly on the inside therefore I'm ugly on the outside.
My heart is broken; therefore, I am broken,
broken down into little pieces like a puzzle with no visible picture.
I cry on the inside,
and my tears spring forth like a river, a dam has been broken and the tears
    just flow.
My pain is internal,
and I smile no more.
What once was golden is now rusted and old.
My world once spun; now it's stopped cold.
What once I did in glory, now's done in vain.
Happiness was the norm, now in its place
only pain.

TWO WORDS

We've been together for two years strong,
through the ups and downs,
the good, bad and the ugly, and the merry-go-rounds.

We've been together,
going at it like rabbits in the woods, no gloves, just love.
Truth is, the shit was good!
I loved you like no other could. You were my end-all be-all.
But things have changed, cause I got two words for you . . .

I'm Pregnant!
I'm holding in my womb all the hate for you that I've consumed from this
    two-year turmoil.
The things you've done,
the words you've spoken,
all left me heartbroken,
but you were able to plant your seed.

It fused with all the rejection and lack of affection I've received.

So we've conceived!

And it clings to my walls, fertilized by the boiling blood of the infidelity
    I accepted
and the common sense I rejected.
So I'm Pregnant!

I'm bearing this child built out of lies, hurt, deceit, and pain.
I'm Pregnant,
but I won't be for long.
I'm due to give birth any day now.
My body is about to be rid of all these feelings

and, after I give birth,
I got a trick for you:
I'm done!
And I'm leaving our baby with you.

WHY DIDN'T I SEE IT COMING?

Why didn't I see it coming?
Why didn't I prepare?
The seasons were changing, and I wasn't even aware.
Now I'm standing here, naked and bare,
a sight for all the world to stare.
Shit doesn't go right.
I know it's true cause otherwise I wouldn't be sitting here feeling so blue.
So out of place in my own environment,
steady wanting to cry and vent
my anger that I hold deep inside,
holding it back so I can hide the hurt and pain I feel,
but I know the deal.
The seasons have changed, and I have to prepare for the cold,
prepare for the lack of the warmth I had when I had you to hold.

HEAVEN IS THE WAY

Heaven is the way it feels to be held in your arms late at night.

Heaven is the way you say my name gently, softly, slowly when we're
   pressed body to body, soul to soul.

Heaven is the way you caress my body. Gliding your hands over my skin.
   Exploring and touring what you already know is yours.

Heaven is the knowing look in your eyes when our eyes meet. Looking at me
   as if you can see into my mind, interpreting all the thoughts and feelings
   I have for you.

Heaven is what it feels like being held in your arms late Sunday night, safe
   from harm.

But where am I when I'm not with you?

I'VE CRIED

I've cried.
Because the pain went deep, and my sorrow was my burden to carry alone.
I've cried.

Because I've lost the most important thing to me, and no one's around to
give me sympathy.
I've cried.

Because the blue skies turned grey, and I'd lost my way and was to be
forever lost within the bleak darkness of hell.

I've cried
because my joy was so real, I wore a smile everyone could feel.

JUST THE THOUGHT OF YOUR NAME DRIVES ME INSANE

Just the thought of your name drives me insane, but now thoughts of you
    are all in vain.
From the passion we once shared, I could tell love was once there.
But now, nevermore.

Yet it is you I still adore,
wanting to kiss your sweet lips and recapture that feeling of pure bliss that I
    received each time I lay in your arms.

So I sit and pray, hoping that you'll see that everything you desire in a
    woman is in me and one day we'll finally rejoice in our unity and the
    completion of We.

HOW DID I END UP IN THIS PLACE?

How did I end up in this place?
Torn, confused, not knowing which lover to choose,
hoping that, in the end, I'll make the right decision.
I know that one treats me better,
so here I sit and write this letter, this poem, this song,
because I know not which path to choose,
because either one would be terrible to lose.

My heart tells me I know exactly what to do.
It's my mind that's putting me through this abuse.
These feelings I have I've never felt before,
these feeling I have I want to explore,
but still,
I have to choose between two friends.

YOU

You,
I yearned for you.
You got way further than my skin;
you got into my soul.
You went deep within and stirred feelings.
I had no control.
You,
you were the one to make me laugh.
You were there when I was sad and feeling lost.
I ache for that feeling again,
the feeling of knowing that in you I had a friend.
You,
you were the one who brightened my day.
You made my divided world entwine.
You made the planets align
just to put a smile on my face.
Now that love is gone, and the world is too cold,
naked and bare, I stand here waiting for your return.
But that'll never be because you've left me.
You're standing by His side in all His grace and glory
while I'm left here to mourn and tell your story,
your legacy,
about how you loved me with all your heart
and how only death did us part,
about how we were meant to be, but
God needed you more than me.
Your passionate kisses, your reluctant smile, your caring eyes, your gentle
   touch
I'll forever keep in my heart.
So go . . . for now.
Goodbye, Sweetheart.

ME

Me
All these thoughts flowing through your brain
no one understands your pain.
You sit on the side, taking it all in stride. Meanwhile, no one knows you're
    quietly dying inside.
You yourself don't understand what exactly you're going through, but you
    feel confused with all that's happening around you.
You want to scream and shout, curse somebody out.
You want to rebel, yell, tell everyone to go to hell.

Yet you don't.

You quietly sit on the side holding all that inside,
helping others out when you're the one who needs help,
hoping they'll see your arms stretched out invisibly,
looking, searching for someone who can reach inside
and know the feelings that you hide and all the thoughts that you conceal
and know the things you want to reveal but are afraid to because that's just
    not you.

You're the strong one who helps others through their trials.
You're not allowed to feel the same way they do.
You're not allowed to be confused or feel pain.
Someone has to be there to keep everybody on the straight and narrow.
You're not allowed to stray from the path.
You have to keep the pack together.
You are the strength of the group.
Yet you feel like you need to be alone,
or you yearn for someone to conquer your soul.
Someone to look deep inside and see
ME.

MRS. DARCY

It fell from the corner of my eye and blurred my vision so that the world was
  unclear.
It trekked its way down the contours of my face, cascading down my cheek,
  dangling at my jaw, finally puddling in the crease of my neck,
staining my face and leaving visible to all its path and, even worse,
  its existence.
No other followed because I soon controlled my heart,
but somehow this one escaped.
It unleashed itself from the tightly held reins of my controlled emotions and
  slipped cunningly out the side door,
visible for all the wrong reasons.
Betraying all the words that escaped my lips and belying the utter truth,
my pain ran deep and with every word spoken I was cut to the quick.
But even though I held tight,
oh so tight, how tightly I held,
one slipped out and fell,
leaving in its trail the final unadulterated truth:
I have loved you, now love you, and will forever always love you.

WHERE'D IT ALL GO?

Where'd it all go?
At one point in time, your love was all mine.
It consumed me, empowered me, nurtured me, made me whole.
It came from deep within your soul.
You gave it willingly and freely but now it's those words, those feelings that
   you choose to withhold.

So where'd it all go?
Did the love you have for me vanish into thin air?
Is it really possible that the love I once felt just isn't there?
Or is it hidden way down deep beneath the surface,
buried in your heart of hearts?
Has it become a planted seed waiting to be nurtured and watered with my
   love and presence,
a budding blossom waiting to bloom so that once again it can emerge
and consume me, empower me, and make me whole?
Seriously, the love we once had for each other,

where'd it all go?

LOVE IS MUSIQ

Sitting patiently waiting . . .

for the seconds, minutes, hours, and days to pass when I'm in your arms
again.

AT LAST! Like *Etta James.*

Your absence is a continuous pain

in my heart,

my limbs,

my brain.

Your presence is better than **Novocain** after an evicted tooth.

My love has more **TRUTH** than *Beanie Siegel* before his conviction and his
stint in the pen.

My home is just a den, a desk, and some chairs without your tender grace.

I can't wait till we bless my crib, my home, my place which will soon be our
castle with you as my king,

and once you get your freedom, you will reign supreme,

and all the court jesters who've been courting your queen will bow down
because you're

back and **PAPA DON'T TAKE NO MESS** like *James Brown.*

And it will be me, Sherell, who restores your crown upon your regal scalp,

and damn all those who doubt that our love is true or that we could get
through anything!

Everything!

Because through the ups and downs, whether we were on the outs, I'm your
queen and our relationship has more **U.N.I.T.Y** than *Ms. Owens* ever
rapped about,

and though they may chat about our love,

it's better than **GETTING LIFTED** like *John* or a **COOKOUT** with *Missy,*

cause, unlike the rest of them, we don't have beef like *Game* or *50,*

and our love isn't shifty like the fault lines of Cali

but steady and fruitful like the coal mines in Africa that produce better
diamonds than the R.O.C

and let it be known that, like *Jay*,
I WILL NOT LOSE!
Our love will stand the test of time
and in my heart,
my soul,
my body,
and my mind,
you will always be mine,
forever and always.

LOVE IS MUSIQ

BILLY'S DAUGHTER

I thought I had more time,
time to reconnect, to let you meet us, to get to know us
and to love us.
I thought we had more time.
I wanted to meet you and tell you to your face that I loved you anyway.
Despite the distance and time and lack of physical presence,
I LOVED YOU!
I thought about you, wondered what you would think of the decisions
   I've made.
How you would feel knowing you're a grandfather, abuelo?
I thought I had more time, but it's too late and we never got to meet again.
I never got to tell you my hopes and dreams and let you comfort me when
   I feel lost and I thought that I would be found if I found you.
I wanted to tell you so much,
wanted you to know so much.
I guess you know everything now, being Heaven bound.
But the most important thing I've ever wanted you to know,
to say to your face, was this:
Even though we haven't been face to face in decades, you've always held
   a place in my heart.
I'll love you Always.

LA HIJA DE BILLY

Yo pensé que tendríamos más tiempo,
tiempo para conectarnos, tiempo para vernos, tiempo para llegar
    a conocernos
y tiempo para amarnos.
Yo pensé que tendríamos más tiempo;
quería conocerte y decirte que a pesar de todo
TE AMO!
Yo pensaba en ti, me preguntaba ¿qué pensarías tú sobre las decisiones que
    he tomado?
¿Cómo te sentirías al saber que eres abuelo, grandpa?
Yo pensé que tendría más tiempo, pero es muy tarde y nunca volvimos
    a vernos.
Yo nunca llegue a decirte mis esperanzas y sueños para que tú pudieras
    confortarme tal vez
cuando me sentía perdida y pensé que me encontraría al encontrarte a ti.
Yo quería decirte tanto,
quería que supieras tanto,
me imagino que ahora lo sabes todo camino al cielo.
Pero lo más importante que siempre quise que supieras
y decirte frente a frente fue esto:
Que, aunque no pudimos vernos frente a frente en décadas, tú siempre
    ocupaste un lugar en mi corazón.
Te amo por Siempre.

II

ON THIS DAY I RISE AND VOW TO CHANGE THIS MOMENT, THIS MINUTE, THIS HOUR

On this day I rise and vow to change this moment, this minute, this hour.
I vow to be all the things capable of me.
I vow to live my life in pure respect.
I vow to never regret.
I vow to always make time to watch the sun set, to listen to the birds sing,
    to let my voice ring
loud and clear
so everyone can hear
that I am pure and so sure that the life given to me will not be wasted on
    desperate things
and foolish dreams.
I will cherish every moment, every breath, every second.
This I vow!

MY LOVE

Forget the pots of gold, I'll give you my love eternally.
This, you'll see, is all you'll ever need.
I'll love you in death, I'll love you in life,
we could be husband and wife.
Very soon you'll see my love is all you need.

My hugs will mean the world.
My kisses you will adore.
My touch will set you afire. I'll be what you desire.
My smile will bring you more happiness than any diamond you possess.
My knowledge you will enjoy.
Our heartfelt talks will be your toys.
Never underestimated the power of my love.
That's the best gift from the Lord above.
Your possession of me is all you'll ever need.

You need not ask, come with me.
I'm always there standing by your side.

You're at the altar, I'm your bride.
I'll never beg you to come my way.
I give you my thoughts, I give you my heart.
For this, in return, we'll never part.
I give you reasons to go on.
I am your sunrise and sunset.
With me you'll never regret.
The light I give to your day brightens the world in every way.
What I'm trying to say is
my world is yours, and our love is here to stay.

THINK BEFORE SPEAKING

I said to myself . . . I think I love this man!
Whew! To get that boulder off my chest.
But I thought again, and I know better.
If I indeed loved him, it wouldn't be a thought.

I would be consumed by this feeling.
I would be surrounded by an inexplicable desire to express this feeling.
If I loved him,
he would know.
He would look at me and see it in my eyes, my demeanor,
my every move toward, about, and near him would exude the raging fire
   of my love.
I just like him a lot.
Whew! Glad I cleared that up before I said something stupid.

TIME SPENT WITH YOU IS A GENTLE BREEZE

Time spent with you is a gentle breeze,
pure, refreshing, satisfying.

The things you do to me are prayers God has answered,
so welcome and desired.

HIS VOICE IS SOOTHING

His voice is soothing,
running through the ocean,
flowing through the room and controlling my vibe.
His words are
warm caresses on my ears,
tingling, tantalizing, seductive.
His whispers
gently raise the hairs on my arms with their promises.
He engulfs me. I surrender.

Our worlds merge.

He is I, and I am he.
We become one, but our union is different.
It is he who controls my mood.
He who dictates my feelings,
and I allow it. I yearn for it, my mind body and soul calling for it.
Our motives are different,
but we're on the same path to the climax of our day.

The song now nears its end,
and I exhale.

KISSING YOU

If every night were a perfect night, what would it be . . .
Would it be me kissing you and you kissing me?
Would it include romance, love, and passion displayed unabashedly,
all eyes on us as we touch and kiss our pains away,
seeking boundless pleasure untold,
our true purpose of this night yet to unfold?

All eyes on us,
they can tell,
enraptured, engaged eyes pointed and fixed.
They watch as we ignite our souls.
Unified bliss,

our worlds collided, divided and, once again, we exist

once our lips touch,
as soon as we kiss.

THE BEAUTY OF MY HEART GOES DEEP

The beauty of my heart goes deep,
and that is something no man can control.
My sex you question because you just don't know
that it's something worthy to behold.

My lips, my eyes, my breasts, my hair,
all add to my flair, my style, my glory, my grace.

That's why I always have men in my face,
questioning *am I real?*
Can I be?
A woman so beautiful, could I possibly not know
that I hold their hearts in my hands
and could have the gall to stand there
with the poise and the stance of
A MAN.

MY OPTIONS

Failure is not an option.
For if I fail, I am limited;
things are put out of my reach, or so they say.

I'm young and ambitious.
I'm not supposed to have fears.
I'm supposed to be courageous and headstrong.
Insecure and scared are not in my vocabulary,
at least that's what they tell me.

The truth is, I don't care what you think about my options.
I'm allowed to be scared and insecure.
I'm allowed to have fears.
I'm supposed to feel these things and more.

I'm not limited, because I choose not to fail.

YOU WANT ME

I have no ass,
wide legs,
a crooked smile,
and no sense of style.

Yet You Want Me.

I cannot see you coming from a distance,
my voice is a little deep, rather raspy.
My feet are big, and my toes are ugly.

Still, You Want Me.

You tell me I'm smart, respectable, and nice.
You say my legs are beautiful, and my height is just fine.
You say my voice is a soothing glass of fine wine after a long day.

And Yes! You Still Want Me

You say there's no need to look into the distance,
because you'll always be standing right next to me.
You say my crooked smile is all you ever want to see,

Because You Want Me.
My body is perfect from my head to my toes.
My mind is beautiful and so is my soul.
My heart is forever flowing with love,
and it's because of those things most of all that

YOU WANT ME.

CAUGHT ETERNALLY BETWEEN

Caught eternally between
Wants and Needs,
Physical over Emotional Joys,
Pleasure and Pain,
Contentment over Eternal Happiness,
Life over Death.

You see Love, Happiness, and Life in the far distance;
you walk towards them, but they move farther away.

Yet Pain, Contentment, and Death move closer.

I'm Lazy.

THE CONSTRAINTS OF A WOMAN LIKE ME

The constraints of a woman like me
are tightly bound with little alleviation of pain.
They cut into the skin, slowly pressing tightly,
squeezing out my power and knowledge and the reasons why I go on.

The captors of a woman like me are cruel, merciless, cold-hearted fools,
for they know not of what a woman like me can bring them.

The woman they are constraining,
the woman I am, is quiet.
What is it about me that scares them?

I'm powerful,
bold,
and I hold my knowledge deep within,
unyielding to their forms of torture and pain.

The possibility of another woman like me is finding one turquoise strand in
    a field of wheat,
yet I feel her presence.
Her shadow lies beneath my very own.

So if by chance my captors feel they are done with me and think there are
    no other women
like me out there, they are mistaken.
She stands in the darkest shadows,

just as quiet,
just as bold,
just as powerful.

HOPE ETERNAL

In a world filled with improbabilities and impossibilities, I found you.
Safe and secure, entombed in a womb of security, shielded from all pain and
    fear
and the unpleasantness that exists just because.
In the midst of my turmoil and confusion, bloody and torn, from the many
    fusions and divisions of me and him and her and them,
missing vital pieces
in the midst of all this,
you, precious, it's you I found.

I was glad.

You existed and survived through my darkness,
deeply encased within the confines of my sore and bleeding heart,
never to leave. With me from the start and outlasting them all, sustaining
    me through the pains of the many stumbles, trips, and falls my body took.
Safe from all the pieces torn away from lovers and loved ones who weren't
    meant to stay.
There you were
safe, encased deeply within my heart.
The girl inside the woman who still believed,
the girl inside the woman, you were not deceived by all the world's
    improbabilities
and impossibilities and you knew that everything wouldn't stay dark
    for long, because it wasn't meant to be.
This girl inside the woman is *Hope*, eternally.

MY REASON

I gotta go so I'm not the only one holding on.
And for what reason?
So I gotta go.
I'ma leave now before I cry some more tears cause if I don't, I'll be the only
    one crying.
And for what reason?
So I'm leaving now.
Because we have nothing left and, after seven tumultuous years, if I were
    to stay, I'll be the only one left with a broken heart.
And for what reason?
I'm gone
so that I can give my heart, joy, and happiness to someone who can give me
    the same.
That's my reason.

TEN DAYS CAN FEEL LIKE AN ETERNITY

Ten days can feel like an eternity.
Did you ever want something so bad you
couldn't eat,
couldn't sleep,
couldn't concentrate on the task at hand
cause all your thinking is you miss ya man?
The way he says your name,
how he looks into your eyes,
how his hands caress your skin,
how even his voice is so strong.

Oh my God, the days are long when I'm not in his arms.
When he grabs my neck and kisses my lips,
when he places his hands upon my hips and holds me close,
oh this is what I miss the most,
being in his embrace and feeling secure that in this moment in time he is
    truly mine
and in my arms is where he wants to be
because he too knows that ten days can feel like an eternity.

WELL WHAT DO YOU WANT? HE ASKS

Well, *what do you want?* he asks.
Nobody has ever asked me that, I reply.
All they've done is take and take
and needed and pleaded for me to fulfill their dreams and fantasies,
coddle their souls, give of my mind, for me to be their precious gold . . .
   a trophy,
my body the ambrosia feeding the gods. And, stupid me,
I continue to feed them, egging on their pride, feeding their souls.
Only to be Denied!
So what you want? he asks.
I don't even know.
I want to bury him in clichés:
I want joy,
I want to be taken care of,
I want to be happy,
I want to love and be loved,
I want to look over and see the key to my lock,
I want to feel complete,
I want you inside of me,
I want you to understand without being told,
I want to whisper secrets in your ear,
I want to be able to reveal my deepest fears,
I want comfort when I'm in pain,
I want to be held in your arms and feel safe from harm.
But, most of all, I want you to want me, wholly, fully, completely.
So, do you know? he asks.
I'll have a number one with bacon, extra mayo, coke no ice, I reply.

IF YOU WERE HERE . . . RIGHT NOW

If you were here . . . right now during this moment of how I'm truly feeling
   you would understand
the passion and fire buried deep inside of me, and you would not only
   be pleased, but blessed
with the knowledge of the power I possess that only the worthy have
   witnessed.
Alas . . . Atlas, you're busy holding up the Heavens.

HE IS SOFT WHERE YOU ARE HARD

I.

His kisses mean nothing.
His touch means nothing.
His presence is tolerated.
He lies in your place.
He looks foreign, an object misplaced.

I want to move him.
He doesn't feel right.
His scent fills my nose, permeates my skin;
I can taste it on my tongue.
It's all wrong,
and that doesn't feel right,
smell right,
taste right.
Everything is wrong.
He takes up space where u belong.

II.

And just like that, you were there
in your spot. Your snores were familiar. Your scent was not only tolerable
    but inviting. Your presence wasn't a nuisance. You were hard where you
    always were.
You were hairy in the typical places.
You lay in your spot and, even though you were asleep, you were still more
    engaging
than the perpetrator who intended to take your place.
It's crazy,
I know.
I see

in this space,
in my place
within these walls,
the universe is telling me
you belong with me.

ONE OF MANY . . .

When will they see there is only just one me,
supreme and spectacular in my being,
never boring, never lame?
Even if every day was just the same,
the masses wouldn't be needed.
Those others should beg and plead to get the attention that they seek.
Yet you are weak, never understanding what you truly got at home,
always on the roam, the hunt, the prowl, for extra bitches
whose wish is to steal my crown,
take my place,
unseat me from my throne.

But honey, I am laughing all the way
cause I refuse to beg a nigga to stay.
Let him free to do what he does;
the most deserving will receive my love.
A man that doesn't see the emerald that I am is not my man,
can't even be a friend.

What would I look like standing around letting a no good nigga make me
    frown,
cry,
or feel less than
the Queen, the crown, the jewel
that I am?

YOU HAVE NO IDEA ABOUT THE BURDENS SHE CARRIES

You have no idea about the burdens she carries,
the things she's done,
the tasks she's undertaken,
the lines she's stood on,
the arguments she's had,
the lies she's believed,
the truths she's told,
the meetings,
the arrangements,
the sleepless nights,
the endless days,
the sacrifices she makes every day,
putting back what she needs to fulfill your wants.

You have no clue
about the dues she's paid,
the roads she's paved,
the hurdles she's jumped,
and you never will.
All you will ever see is her smile.

WHAT THE FUCK IS GOING ON?

What the fuck is going on?
Catching feelings so strong
you got me wanting to be in your arms forever.
Beyond sexual healings,
you give me good feelings,
helping me learn the truth in a way only you can.
Spitting rhymes from ya temple,
Babygirl, I'm feeling ya mental.

Sexual chemistry is getting me hot in my zone.
When we bone, it's on and only nosy niggas stop us from getting proper.
Cause I could wake the dead when you giving me head,
but I bite my lips slow and give you a moan.
Babygirl, when I'm with you, it's on,
so come on home.

WOULD YOU

Would you crisscross straight through hell for me?
Would you steal for me?
Would you kill for me?
Would you lie for me?
Would you die for me?
Would you sit down and have a good cry for me?
Would you believe in me?
Would you stomp a hater down just to be with me?

Can you see with me all the future holds
with just you and me?

IF YOU'VE EVER CARED

If you've ever cared,
if you've ever revealed your heart and soul,
if you've ever exposed your deepest fears and darkest desires,
if you've ever loved and had it thrown in your face,
been made to feel a fool about the love you gave,
the secrets you revealed,
the things you did and said that took you out of your comfort zone,
if you've ever felt like a complete and utter fool
after you've given your all,
then you did it again.

You're not stupid.
You're no fool.
You are a true lover of love.
You are my hero.

I DON'T WANT TO BE CONQUERED BY LOVE

I don't want to be conquered by love.
I want to be enveloped by a consuming love that inspires my desire to be
    a true woman.
I don't want a love that would pillage my body and spirit,
leaving nothing but hate in its wake and the ruins of a woman
once emblazoned like the sun by the possibilities of love
who is now as desolate and dry as the desert with no hope for rain.

I don't want to be conquered by love.
I want to rejoice in a pure love and sing its praises to the high heavens,
thanking God for surrounding me in HIS purest form.
I don't want a love that I have to sacrifice my wellbeing for,
one that bruises my ego as well as my flesh,
a love that brings pain and distress.
I want a love so blessed the resounding joy in my soul speaks to the masses
and all those listening raise their glasses and toast in support.

YESTERDAY'S PAIN

Never really ever having felt this way before leaves me confused and slightly
    off.
My heart is paying the cost of having surrendered my entire being to you.
Now retribution is due.
I have to pay myself back and love myself more and find the ultimate
    strength
to walk through the door and close it firmly behind me because we're
    through.

Even though I'll always love you,
I have to love me more and try to restore the broken pieces and mend my
    heart so it restarts
fresh and new and I won't feel so bad that I don't have you to hold and touch
    and kiss,
and maybe your presence in my life I will hardly start to miss,
and one day I'll look and find that my heart is indeed intact, and I won't look
    back to yesterday's pain.
I won't feel the same way I do today.
I'll move on, be a better person, and the love we shared won't all have been
    in vain.

STRUGGLE IS OUR STRENGTH

Why are rocks thrown at beautiful beings?
Why do good girls go through bad things?
Why do the strong have to fight so hard?
Why? Oh most forgiving God,
why did my homegirl have to get raped?
Why did she have to feel unsafe
and in her own home, no less?
Why are the bad people so blessed?
Why did my friend have to have an abortion?
Why?
Did she throw caution to the wind?
Did she lack a friend?
Naw, I don't think so.
I'm here forever as a friend.
Why do the strong have to fight so hard?
Why? Oh most forgiving God,
why did my friend, my sister have to make such an important decision,
choosing between her life as a single parent and life as a young college
    student?
Why did the friend I love so much have to go through something so rough,
confused and torn thinking she's in the wrong,
never knowing that she's so strong and that's why she fought so long?
Why do the strong have to fight so hard?
Why, oh most forgiving God?

FIELDS OF COTTON

I see the fields of cotton as I stand in the blazing sun.
I have no idea what I would've done,
my back scarred from the wear and tear of bearing my master's income.
 The fields are hot;
I can't understand how my ancestors did it.
I'm standing here on hallowed ground,
the land on which my ancestors toiled and boiled in this tremendous heat
which scorches and torches the skin, making it hard to battle the demons
 within.
Or is it without?
The white demon
who beat the black man into submission
and made him feel less than human.
But is that true?
Is my king that dude who will be subdued and broken,
reduced to nothing but a token of acceptance?
Repentance for the sins of our forefathers, the true starters of hate and
 torture,
the ones who brought ya to this land of independence to sing and rejoice
 the King.
God the Lord!
The Lord who saves us all and forgives our sins.
The one who would do it over and over and over again to save our souls.
Oh Lord!
Let me be bold and break hold of these chains which hold and reign in my
 attitude
and love and character which I feel are given from up above.
The attitude of determination to terminate the possession I am in,
my place,
my race
is all settled on my shoulders.
But I,

I refuse to let this boulder oppress me and depress me and make me a small
  being.
I stand tall in this field
by this church
with my family and remember,
or is it reminisce about things way back?
I lift my shoulders and un-bow my head and walk with the living dead who
  reside
in me and want me to be more than they ever dreamed to be.
I stand tall because I've answered my call.
I've become the person they dreamed to be:
doctors,
lawyers,
fixers of injustice.
But did I do justice?
Am I diligent,
receptive,
independent
and, most of all, appreciative?
Yes!
I know what I have sacrificed and what was sacrificed for me,
so I do this for thee!
For my ancestors who toiled and boiled and bore the scars of past masters,
those who slaved and cooked and took everything I didn't or wouldn't or
  couldn't
because of the determination, spirit and inspiration instilled in thee.
These lessons have been passed on to me!
Yes! These cotton fields are real to me.

IT'S INEVITABLE

There will come a day when
all that I am and all that I possess,
my greatness
my strength
my love
my resilience
my integrity
my dedication
my Blackness
MY POWER!
will become not only my reality
but yours as well.
I will no longer be
INVISIBLE.

SO WHAT DOES IT MEAN

So what does it mean
when you . . .
give and take,
bend and break,
give and grow
and give some mo'?
What does it all mean
when you . . .
fight and win
and have to fight again?
When you . . .
slave and cook,
teach and learn,
moan and groan,
bleed and heal,
when you feel . . . EVERYTHING!
What does it all mean
when the shadows overtake,
but then they break and the light shines through
and you continue
to give and take,
bend and break,
reap and sow,
give and grow,
love and feel,
hurt and heal,
stand and fall?
What does it mean?
It means . . .
love and pain,
hurt and shame,
work and gain,

tears and fears.
It means . . .
life and love.
It means God is really up above shining on you and seeing you through. . . .
the bending,
the bowing,
the reaping,
the sowing,
the pain,
the work,
the gain,
the giving,
the living,
the growing,
the teaching,
the learning,
and, most of all,
THE LOVE!

AND, EVEN IF MY HANDS WERE FULL WITH ALL MY WISHES AND DESIRES,

And, even if my hands were full with all my wishes and desires,
I would drop them all to embrace you.

CPSIA information can be obtained
at www.ICGtesting.com
Printed in the USA
BVHW070951031220
594763BV00007B/802

9 780578 765303